811

MW00643674

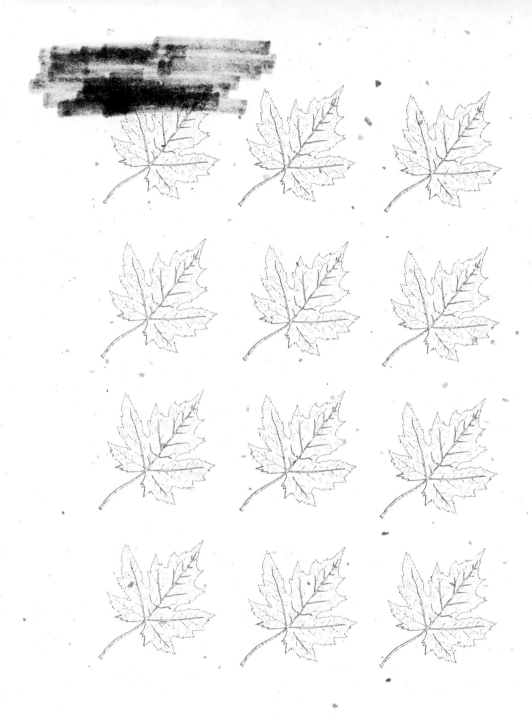

Trees
are the guardians
of the Earth

We
are the guardians
of the trees

-Author Unknown

PoeT❦Tree

The Wilderness I am

Stories and Poems By
Ilan Shamir
and Friends

19 99

Better World Press

Fort Collins, CO

Published by Better World Press
A Division of Your True Nature, Inc.
P.O. Box 272309, Fort Collins, Colorado 80527
800-992-4769 email: grow@yourtruenature.com

Ninth Printing

Original Illustrations by Ilan Shamir
Illustration for "I am the Tree of Life" by Rajan Kose
Public domain images on pages 16, 48, 54, 76
Advice from a Tree is a registered trademark of Your True Nature, Inc.

Stories and Poems used by permission:
          "Redwood Mystery" by Rabbi Zalman Schachter-Shalomi
          "Spruce Tree's Promise" by Kathy Gatewood-Greenbank
          "Plant a Tree - Grow a Friend" by Sheldon Sands & Ilan Shamir
          "Invocation for Earth Day Tree Planting" by Katharine Gregory
          "Beginnings and Endings" by Martha McClennan-Stapp

Library of Congress Cataloging-in-Publication Data
ISBN 1-930175-00-0

          Shamir, Ilan, 1951-
                  PoeTTree : The Wilderness I am / Ilan Shamir
                  1. Trees   2. Poetry   3. Spiritual
                  4.   Human Growth and Potential

Printed in USA on Recycled Paper. Thanks to the trees
for their gift of paper! Paper used in the printing of
this book has been replanted through the 100%
Replanted program. Visit www.ReplantTrees.org

This book is dedicated to:

Kris
who plants love and kindness
in my life and in the lives
of so many others!

Contents

PoeTTree

Stories and Poems by Ilan Shamir

Tree Stories from Friends

Introduction

On my sixth birthday I received many presents. I can remember only one. My Aunt Barbara and Uncle Stanley gave me a Magnolia sapling. Wow, I thought, my own tree! I planted it outside my bedroom window. In some way, I also planted the Magnolia in my heart. It grew into a love of all trees that has become one of the central themes of my life. A simple gift of kindness and beauty, an infant tree, has grown into a lifetime of appreciation and celebration of nature.

The roots of this teaching have spread and taken hold deep inside of me. They have touched a passion for the wild beauty of the human soul, and its connection to the wildness of life: the wilderness *I am*. I have felt my vision reach out as if branches of some great tree that beholds the entire forest from an exalted perch. All is poetry. All is song. Every tree a gift of wonder.

My name, Ilan, means *tree* in Hebrew, Shamir, *protector*. Ilan Shamir, protector of trees . . . of life and of celebration! Many knew me as Scott Alyn before I changed my name four years ago. My friends call me Tree Man! I have been involved in planting somewhere close to fifty thousand trees. I don't intend to stop. Trees are so central to life, so much a theme in our literature and philosophies, I can't think of anything that would bring me closer to the core of who I am. Trees give us shelter, fire for heat and cooking. No Europeans would be in America if generous trees hadn't raised up the hulls and masts of great ships. This very book is inscribed on the breath of trees.

The ancient root of the word tree is *deru*, which means solid, steadfast. The same root, *deru*, generates the words *trust, true* and *truth*. Trees have never let me down. They never fail to inspire. In their presence, I am always led to a deep and intuitive understanding of my place in the living web of life. Small trees remind me to care for the young and tender, to be hopeful for the future. What I breathe out, trees breathe in. What trees breathe out is the fuel of my blood. The colors of leaves and bark, the smell of pine, the shapes in branches, the shimmering of leaves in twilight, all awaken in me an endearing affinity with life and the divine beauty of this planetary jewel we call home.

You can imagine how, along the way, I have accumulated a few stories about trees. In sharing them with others, I began to realize I wasn't alone. Others had trees like my Magnolia. As I listened to their stories, observed their sparkling eyes in the telling, heard their voices youthful and impassioned, an

PoeTTree

immediate bond formed between us. In that instant it felt as if we were enthusiastic Cottonwoods that had been growing just out of site of each other and were lovingly reunited as a rock cliff that hid our view suddenly crumbled. What sort of magic in trees can build a lifelong friendship in a moment? I haven't the answer. I can only delight in the mystery.

Out of this it comes to pass that I have written a book. I call it PoeTTree because in every tree there is a poem, a song, a natural and humble work of art inviting us to behold. I hope, in some small way, it honors the trees I have known. I hope it kindles the spirit of protection and celebration of trees in others. At the very least, for me it is a planting. It is a tender shoot in the soft rich soil of

time that says: I was here, and this is what inspired me. If others can find some inspiration in my words, I would be honored. More importantly, if the trees are treated with a little more kindness, given a little more appreciation, shielded from acts of indifference, something has been accomplished.

The book's format is taken from the forest. Stories, poems, songs and illustrations have been interplanted and create environments for one another. No one form dominates another, and so each is strengthened by the diversity. Furthermore, some pieces such as "Spruce Tree's Promise", "Redwood Mystery" and others are works that have been shared by special tree friends of mine who bring their love of trees to this surprising meander through a wordful woodland.

And so I encourage you to remember your own tree stories. Tell them around a warm dancing wood fire. Thank the tree for the heat. And plant, yes, plant and plant and plant. Give trees to children, encourage them to love the trees. Plant a tree when your child is born. Plant a tree when your mother dies. Give a tree for a birthday present. Like me, I bet whoever receives a tree will remember the gift above all others. Paint a picture. Make a tree movie. Inscribe a poem. Etch your eternal love of another by planting a tree. Go back to that spot and the tree will show you how much you have grown together.

Bringing people who love trees together is an important part of writing this book. If you have a poem, picture or experience you would like to share with this growing collection of tree wisdom, I would heartily welcome hearing from you. I will send you a gift of my appreciation, a beautifully illustrated Advice from a Tree poster.

I am deeply grateful to trees for their endless gifts of luscious green and passionate yellow, their silhouettes against dreamsicle morning skies, for their warmth, and for the shelter they give, to people, birds, childhood and dreams. I am also thankful for their teaching. The Cottonwood reminds us to stand tall. The Willow teaches flexibility. Fluttering leaves remind us to stay loose, flow with the wind! The Maple reminds us to share our beauty. The windswept Pine clinging to a dry rock face asks us to make the most of what we're given. The Aspen groves, with their shared root system, remind us of our interdependent connection, that how, underneath, we are all enriched by the same soil. When trees drop their leaves in fall, they remind us to surrender to the seasons, to give in to nature's way, to cherish what we have, knowing it will pass. Winter snows will cover. Spring runoff will wash away. Summer heat will melt and turn to mist.

I am thankful to those who have planted the trees in the shade I now find comfort. To Johnny Appleseed, John Muir, Gifford Pinchot, Andy Lipkis, the founders of Arbor Day, and the countless thousands who

protected and renewed the forest, wild and urban, I salute you! The footsteps of tree planters are there to help us find our way to turn our passions into action. Find the wilderness *you are*. Seek the wild places near your homes. Embrace trees! They will reassure you when fear crops up in your overtended garden. Explore! Let your limbs sway and dance with the breezes! Climb trees and sit in them like a bird. Read books and turn the pages as if working a pile of leaves. Trees are in every story. Seek the wild places in your soul. Care for the trees there. Make room for your spreading dreams to fully extend. Let there be a reforestation in the human woodland. Let the denuded landscapes find loving hands to plant them anew.

PoeTTree

Plant
Your Words,
Dear Friend,

Like Tender Saplings

So that One Day You Can Stand

Among the Forest

and Hear the Winds
of
Your
Own
Voice

and
Be
Comforted.

The Greatest Gift!

The birthdays of my childhood blend together in a mixture of
cake, presents, songs, games, and laughter. It's not often that a
specific year, let alone one isolated gift, stands out in one's
memory. My sixth birthday is the one that stands taller than the
rest, all because of one special gift. It was a gift not packaged or
wrapped, not bought in a toy store or assembled in a factory. It
came to me complete, whole, beautiful and sacred, not seeking a
place in my toy box, but asking for a home in the earth. Aunt
Barbara and Uncle Stanley had given me a Magnolia tree. I can
recall the first touch of my soft young hands on its pencil-thick
trunk. How alike we were, both of us young, fragile, thin and
barely four feet tall, needing the care of others more mature.
Here I was, just a boy of six, being asked for the first time to be
responsible for another life.

With great pride and excitement, I took the sapling out into the
yard and dug a hole for it outside my bedroom window. I'm sur-
prised nobody got whacked in the head the way I swung the long
shovel handle around wildly, dirt flying and my glee spreading out
just as far. I can't say that I knew or didn't know this digging experience was as much a planting in myself as in the earth. I planted
the Magnolia tree in the soil next to the place I slept and dreamed,
and I also planted that young tree in my heart, and it grew inside of
me as I grew into a man.

I loved the Magnolia the way some kids love a puppy. We grew up

together. I might put on an inch or two in a year, and it would grow
a foot, two feet, and more the taller it got. Each spring I waited
and watched for its jubilant white blossoms to sing the joy of
rebirth. Its tender green leaves, waxy, glistening, opened to the
sun, and in that magical tree way, turned the light into wood, into
thickness and height. In my boyhood wonder, I let the Magnolia
teach me to appreciate the richness of the land and the seasons.
The tree became my diary, documenting the passage of time in its
upward yearning branches and ever more plentiful blossoms. It
taught me to be humble, patient, kind and caring, as loving another
often will do.

I learned compassion from this Magnolia, in the pain of seeing a
friend in trouble and being unable to help. The neighborhood
boys knew how much I cared for the tree. It was something of a
joke to them. One day, as I sat at my bedroom window, some boys
bent the Magnolia until its upper branches touched the ground. I
could almost hear its young trunk snap. I watched helplessly,
trying to hide my tears, while they held down my friend. When they
let go and it sprang back to its full height undamaged, I nearly
shouted. It felt as if my own heart began to beat again after sev-
eral moments in a tight fist. The tears came freely now, a mixture
of joy and relief and sorrow, the first childhood inklings of the
losses I would have to endure.

Through junior high and high school, the tree continued to ad-
vance. Its trunk by then was six inches thick and it stood over
twenty feet tall. We had become adults together! I had cared for it

PoeTTree

with water and mulch and love, and it had shown me a simple dedication to life, the unassuming practice of natural growth. I had planted it as an innocent boy, uncertain of what I could do, who I might be. Every time I looked out my bedroom window and saw the Magnolia reaching ever higher, it was like an enthusiastic teacher cheering me on, telling me I could do anything! When doubt and fear threatened to take me over, the Magnolia always reminded me to believe in myself. Leaving it behind when I went to college was so difficult for me. Trees don't come along, I knew, but I would return for visits whenever I could.

After a few years my parents moved from that home on Meadowood Lane to a new house. One day a letter arrived as letters had done many times before. My Dad shared that he went by to see our old homestead and found the new owners had chopped down my tree. They wanted more light in the yard. I couldn't believe it. The rush of anguish, grief and pain hit me like an ax through the chest. Didn't they know this was no ordinary tree? Didn't they . . . ? Somebody should have called me. I would have had it moved. I would have saved it, no matter the cost. Why didn't . . . ? How was I to place my life now? Against what would I measure my growth? No! Tears mixed with outrage. I planted that tree! You don't just kill a tree. You don't! Isn't it obvious that trees, unlike people, grow stronger with age? You don't just cut them down in their prime. Eventually, I had to accept that it was done. Nothing could bring it back. Nothing.

Sometime after the news of my tree's death, I returned to San

Antonio for a family visit. I saw my Uncle Stanley, who had given me the Magnolia, and shared with him that someone had cut it down and how much I ached inside and missed it so. He took me into his back yard and stood with me in the shade of a huge Magnolia. He smiled at me and pointed to the tree. "Here's your tree. We moved it." Of all the people I knew, Uncle Stanley understood me. His gesture of sympathy brought a measure of satisfaction to the boy in me who wanted his friend back. My Magnolia would never reach the size of this tree, but others would. I could find inspiration in them. I did not have to give up, to tear the roots of the Magnolia from my heart. I could expand and let the roots of all the trees find nourishment in me.

A few years after my uncle's gift of a full-grown Magnolia, he died. I took some solace in the way he went, of natural causes, not cut down in an act of indifference. Certain people and trees and experiences are precious and irreplaceable. Before he died, Uncle Stanley provided the seed money for my greeting card company. Once again, he had seen me deeply, and gave freely in support of my destiny. I can still see him holding that Magnolia sapling when I was six, encouraging me to plant and grow whatever gifts come to me.

Last year I took my daughter Laurel and my wife Kris to enjoy the roots of my childhood home on Meadowood Lane. I loved walking on the grass and seeing so many of my favorite trees. I treasured returning to the welcoming friends I used to climb and sit under to dream of who I would become. "In 1957 this is where I planted my Magnolia tree!" I said. It was a special moment with two of the people I love the most. I shared the joy and beauty it had brought to me and felt the tugging of my heart, wanting my uncle and the tree he so lovingly gave me to be here with us. Loving someone or something so deeply is always a risk . . . a risk worth taking.

No matter what happens in time, the gift of a tree always enriches the heart.

In the spirit of my uncle, in memory of my Magnolia and in honor of my daughter Laurel, I gave her the present of a young Burr Oak tree on her sixth birthday. We invited her special childhood friends over to celebrate and be a part of the planting in our front yard. This rite of passage was a way for her to mark the journey from being a toddler and small child into a girl now going off to school. Six little girls dug the hole for the tree—magically, no one got bonked with the shovel! Perhaps there is a degree of protection afforded to little tree planters everywhere. All the kids excitedly

lent a hand and lowered this Oak into the opening arms of the
Colorado soil. It was an exciting day full of bustling and activity
and in one moment everyone and everything came to a silence—a
pause—Laurel reached into her pocket with her tender hands and
pulled out a couple of small objects . . . her way of travelling from
one stage of life into another. She carefully tucked and cradled a
tiny, well-worn tennis shoe from when she was two and a familiar
diaper pin into the soil close to the roots. Filling the hole with
earth brought tears to my eyes as not only she passed into a new
stage, but I did too. She and her friends mounded up the soil and
watered the oak. Small hands holding small hands they circled
around and each of them spoke encouragement to Laurel and the
tree. They sang songs and danced around in the bright June
sunshine. The girls joined fully and naturally in the ceremony,
though none of them had done anything like it before. Watching
them so full of hope, I recalled my own innocence at the same age.
In just five years, the Burr Oak has grown taller and fuller and my
little girl is knocking at the door of womanhood. I often think of
that little shoe, the joyous memories we have shared and how a tree
has brought all of life closer together.

And so I say to you, when each chance comes your way to give a
gift, give a tree.

PoeТTree

Advice From A Tree

Story of Advice from a Tree

It was one of those difficult days . . . one of those days that tore at the very roots of my being. I just had to get outside to breathe and somehow find a way back to my center, a return to the peace and clarity of my soul. I managed to open the front door and with tears in my eyes, I began to move along the sidewalk, lifting one foot in front of the other without a clue where I was going. Exhausted, I leaned against a huge Cottonwood tree; the deep ridges of the bark held me close. I said, "I've been working for you for many years now, planting thousands of trees, teaching about the miracles of the earth and now I need your help! Can you help me? I need some advice." I felt the tree reach out to me, to wrap me in its branches, to comfort me as I leaned against its steady trunk. This old and wise Cottonwood tree spoke to me with clarity and wisdom. I felt hopeful, renewed, loved and went home and word for word wrote the following caring message from this tree friend.

Dear Friend,

Stand Tall and Proud

Sink your Roots deeply into the Earth

Reflect the Light of a greater source

Think long term

Go out on a Limb

Remember your place among all living beings

Embrace with joy the changing seasons

For each yields its own abundance

The Energy and Birth of Spring

The Growth and Contentment of Summer

The Wisdom to let go like leaves in the Fall

The Rest and Quiet Renewal of Winter

PoeTTree

Feel the wind and the sun

And delight in their presence

Look up at the moon that shines down upon you

And the mystery of the stars at night

Seek nourishment from the good things in life

Simple pleasures
Earth,
Fresh Air, Light

Be content
with your natural beauty

Drink plenty of water

Let your limbs sway
and dance in the breezes

Be flexible

Remember your Roots

Enjoy the View!

Tribal
Thunder

I wasn't made to sit behind a desk all day.

The calls of my ancestors echo through my soul,

Calling me to come hunt, to run, to lean into the wind.

I want to sit with my brothers,

To sing, to feel the fire and the earth,

To drum and chant the songs of the land and seasons.

I want to dig into the earth and plant seeds,

To feel the wind and sun on my back.

My knife is dull and rusty,

My digging stick is whittled down to a pencil,

And the wildness stirs ever stronger.

I hear the ancestors calling,

Come,

Let's dance again.

Bring your brothers.

Carry your father, for he longs to dance too.

PoeT Tree

Cottonwood
Vision Quest
Tree

PoeTTree

Our native ancestors knew the power of returning to nature and asking through prayer for guidance into purpose and destiny. They understood the need to release daily concerns to the spirit of the wind, rocks, trees and sky—into the great mystery. And so men and women have left their routines for thousands of years to be alone in a quest for clarity and vision. Thankfully, I had been touched by this practice and its power. I valued the tradition of renewal and the process of winning again and again the advances of soul and virtue by tenderly opening my heart. I was about to do it again.

"Hey, Tree Man," Leav called out. It felt good to be known in that way. "Soon," she continued, "it will be time for your group to choose your vision quest sites." The commanding escarpment of red and white sandstone, carved for millions of years by the winding river, awaited our footsteps. Our experienced leaders, Leav, Jed and Burke, had provided compassionate guidance and wise counsel. They drew upon an extraordinary body of wisdom and experience as ten of us spent three powerful days together releasing, strengthening, sharing our life stories—preparing ourselves for our solo quests. I felt the power and comfort of sitting in a circle with others around the fires of our dreams and passions. Once again I realized how foolish it is to imagine we have to do such things alone. I could also sit in the paradox that for four days I would be alone, and the others would be alone too, yet we were also connected, and stronger in our solitude because of it.

Without food in our backpacks, our mini group, Carol, Christina and I, set out as the sun was rising over the east canyon wall. The warmth of the sun's reflection on the west canyon features called us onward. We surveyed the land with all of our senses as we walked deeper into this remote Utah canyon, each listening for our solo site to call us in. Our footsteps were no longer measured in miles, but in realizations and richness. I laughed as I found myself getting tense and worried about finding just the perfect site. I remembered once again that it was as much about the way I found my site as it was the site itself!

Each of us needed some way to know the other two were okay, yet still remain alone. We were advised to use a simple form of communication involving stones. A smooth, rounded boulder next to the trail seemed the perfect place. We each set a stone in one of the sandy-bottomed hollows on top of this five-foot-high mountain piece well worn by time. Christina would move her stone with the morning sun. Carol would arrive with noon, make sure Christina's rock was shifted, then shift her own. I would trail the afternoon sun, make sure that Carol's rock was moved, and then move mine. Christina would come the next morning and so the cycle would continue for the four days. In this way, we would keep track of each other and preserve the solitude of our quest.

With our rocks in place, we joined hands and wished many blessings and much fullness upon each other. We honored the journeys of others in our group perched and tucked throughout the miles of this wilderness. It was now time for each of us to turn and walk alone in the direction that our hearts led. Alone in the wilderness! I quickly dropped into the cherished tranquility that welcomes me so readily whenever I am in such places. Joy and longing were now my travelling companions. I fell into the awareness of space and the purpose of my journey: to find the place for my vision quest. I wandered up the ancient river bed, drawn upstream like a spirited salmon that seeks its birthplace. True to my name and my calling, the journey ended at the foot of a tree. Once again, a special and remarkable tree, this time a mighty Cottonwood, touched my heart. I knew this would be home for the next four days.

I looked up into the branches of this grandfather Cottonwood, felt its rough bark so deeply grooved, and took in its grandeur. One of the largest upper forks of the massive trunk was broken off, perhaps by wind or lightening or simply age. This tree grew square in the riverbed, pounded by boulders, holding debris of rising waters in its bark. The tree held on with tenacious roots and determination to survive. It had taken from the same boulders that hammered at it and the water that pulled on it the minerals and nutrients to grow so tall and strong. I couldn't help noticing the unusual gnarled branch structure of this old canyon sentinel.

As I stood by the tree to begin speaking the intentions of my journey here a bit of humor surfaced . . . . Buddha spent forty days and nights under the Bodhi tree and found enlightenment. I figured I would spend four days and nights under this Cottonwood tree and at least get a little smarter! Instinctively, I pulled a prayer rattle from my pack. The Huichol Indians had given me this gourd rattle. I shook it and let flow the words of deep gratitude. "Great mighty Cottonwood tree, I honor you. I delight in you. I find comfort in your beauty. I arrive here with my life, with my hopes and dreams, with an open heart to the stars and infinite possibilities and the beauty of who I am! I stand tall at the doorway to my future. For four days and nights I rest my soul in your mighty presence!" East of the tree, against a rock slab, I traced out a circle in the river sand—a medicine wheel, a ceremonial circle taught to me by Native Americans as a way to honor the directions and to hold my intentions and prayers. This would be my home, a sacred hoop of welcome to receive my prayers.

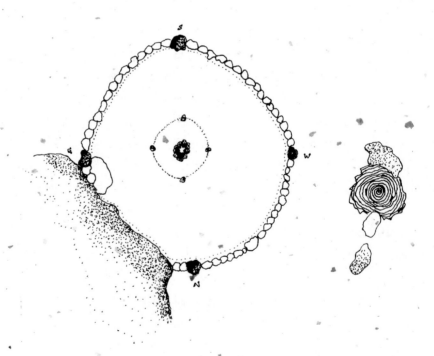

I shook the rattle fiercely from the south point of the circle, raised a smooth river stone and prayed with the words of my heart: "To the SOUTH, place of the midday sun, place of play and nurturing, the fullness of life, I honor and welcome you." I placed the stone solidly in the sand. I moved around the circle. "I honor the WEST, home of the setting sun, the place of letting go and the season of fall." I was there to release, to let die some old ways that no longer served. In turning to the north, the memory of our base camp came to mind. "To the NORTH, place of wisdom and knowing, season of winter and the deepness of mystery, reminder of the wisdom that is always here inside of me, I honor you and invite you to be with me on my quest." "EAST, place of new beginnings and vision, place of hope and bright possibilities, of light and lightness and the season of spring, I honor with you my life in its newness and gifts, I welcome you and invite your presence on my journey," as I placed the fourth stone. I turned to the sky. As I gazed into the leaves of this mighty Cottonwood and beyond to the clear blue expanse, I said: "To the ABOVE, pathway of father sun and sister moon, pathway of hopes and dreams, of rainbows and our winged friends, I feel your blessing and invite your presence." I gently lowered on my knees to the earth and said: "To the BELOW, our mother earth and its many blessings, source of our growing food and path we walk gently upon, I ask you to be with me here on my journey and I welcome you." Finally, I looked inward and spoke: "To the place of the HEART, inner beauty and guidance, the fullness of love, I feel your love and welcome you here today."

PoeTTree

From this sacred circle I wondered what it must have been like for a Cottonwood sapling, now grandfather tree, to shoot up here more than a hundred years ago. Surely it must have endured times that only this tree could tell. How had it survived to grow so tall? What kind of terrible storm had broken off its arms and carried them in a swirling soup of sediment, twigs and leaves down to the valley below? I watched this tree in morning light, twilight, moonlight and starlight, every kind of light, even the iridescent glow of a dream. My kinship with it deepened and broadened with each passing day, each nuance brought out by the various lights that shined on it. It began to feel as if we grew together, that we had been planted at the same time, and what had taken it one hundred years had taken me just forty. The green leaves turned more golden by the minute. A whole new spectrum of color and mood swept through me.

My artistic longing called on me to draw this magnificent tree. The only piece of paper large enough was the map I had been given of the canyon. I turned it over and began to sketch. In following even more closely the shadows and knots of the trunk, the shimmering leaves and twists of limb and branch, I became closer still to this strange, enchanting Cottonwood. As I completed the sketch and looked more closely at the pattern of growth, I suddenly saw a mirror of my own life. Each of the major limbs represented primary aspects of my journey: education, relationships, family, children, and so on. The breaks and bends in the limbs coincided identically with the major changes in my life. The strong and true growth expressed my successes. In its steady quiet way, this tree held my life. In its branches it expressed where I had come, and where I was

40

PoeTTree

going. A cool wind came down the canyon and went straight up my back. I stood face to face with a special and mighty tree—the tree of my life.

A deep stirring of ancient power awakened and inspired me. I sensed how so much had gone by, but in many ways life had just begun. I could see that I was just beginning to blossom into who I am to be. The temptation to look back couldn't compete with the teaching of this tree. I had come here with my aching for direction and guidance. I had come because of a longing for something, a discomfort with tameness and sameness. The tree seemed to know this and had been waiting through the ages for me to arrive.

With the fullness of my heart I prayed to the directions with dedication, asking humbly for guidance on how I could share my many talents and be well received by others. Emotions flooded in like this river filled beyond its banks. I could only think of the tree and how it held on. I had led others on vision quests, and I never doubted that it would work for them. But this was my journey. I was the one who wanted clarity for my life ahead.

What was the matter? Why wasn't I getting it? The light in the tree that had formerly inspired me now seemed to taunt me. It danced my defeat on that sunrise of day four. I offered prayers to the directions and now released them. I thanked the beautiful tree, certain it sneered at me for my failure. My time there was over. All seven of us would rendezvous at the base camp and share our experiences. I shuffled along the dusty trail, weak with hunger. No vision. No clarity. What did I do wrong? I must not have prayed hard enough. Defeat walked with me. All these miles and days of preparation and fasting and I would have to go home and wrestle with the same clouded dilemma of where my life was headed.

We were received with loving open arms and an amazing purification gateway. We were seen and held as a blessing as we gathered around the circle. Carol, Christina, Todd, Shelley, Michaella, Maya, Tree Man . . . all of us dusty, tired and yet alive in a new and deep way. We danced and shared our stories that night with gratitude for the many gifts each of us had been given. I wanted to be ok with the many remarkable gifts of my quest, but disappointment stirred like restless embers of the ceremonial fire.

The next day we packed our things and drove to Glenwood Springs for a soak and good-byes. Even the hot water, the steam and smell of sulfur, couldn't wash the disappointment from me. As we released hands in our closing circle, I felt lost and vulnerable. Walking to my car to leave, I heard a voice call, "Ilan. Ilan, wait." It was Carol, who had taken the name Butterfly. She said, "Ilan, I almost forgot to tell you. I was out in the canyon on my vision quest and it came to me that I wanted to commission a special art piece to hang in my new home and remind me of this spiritual awakening that has been so powerful for me. I want *you* to create this art for me." I began to cry and my legs trembled. Here was the answer. The Cottonwood had been trying to tell me this when it called me to sketch it. The tree must have been laughing now at my earlier disappointment.

With Butterfly's request, the vision spread out before me, a sublime panorama of creativity and art, poetry and ritual. Eventually the vision grew into a practice of using art in story-telling. I named the process, Soul Reflections, and it has helped many see and appreciate their exquisite beauty and unique soul's journey. In my heart, I often return to the canyon and that prophetic Cottonwood and bow down in thanks for the exquisite teaching. I imagine it has a new bend or shoot to represent the vision it inspired. Perhaps one day I will return in person and we will have a good laugh together.

43

PoeTTree

The
Wilderness
I Am

I am

a dedicated preservationist,
committed to protect,
preserve and live my wide,
wild open spaces.

To unravel and unwind
the politics of my doubt and fear.

I grasp
the power
of my nature,
the wildness
and holiness
that I am.

PoeTTree

The chariot of my fire and passion
rides upon the winds of my soul and solitude.

The powerful
and raging rivers
of my blood roar
through my body
with joy and beauty!

It Is
This Wilderness I Am!

Exquisite.
Pristine. Unique.

The Spring, Summer,
Fall, and Winters
of my life
connect me
with the sacred circle.

I Am the soaring Red-tail Hawk on circling
canyon winds,
I Am the guardian Redwood,
The Wild Horse and
Thunder on the plains

J Am
the Call of the Earth!

The
Octopus Tree

The young man's invitation to see an amazing tree caught more than my attention. It caught my imagination, my hopes and my vision of a whole and healthy wilderness. To me, every tree is amazing, and every bush and wildflower and lichen-covered rock. Every so often, though, a truly remarkable presence stands out in the splendor. I hopped into the young man's black pickup without hesitation, and found myself winding through a steep and narrow road in the Oregon coastal range. The rhythm of bumps and bends entranced me. Soon I found myself transported to a similar journey taken ten years ago in the back of a vegetable truck on my way to a remote Huichol Indian village in the mountains of Mexico. Mystery accompanied me on both journeys. In each case, I trusted my guides to lead me deeper into the embrace of wilderness. This was old green, dangling moss, lush, ripe, pungent decay, thick, so the sun had to work hard for a glimpse of the ground. The truck swam a choppy breast stroke through a green-gray pool of fog and mist. Suddenly the truck stopped with a jerk from Eric setting the parking brake. He jumped out of the driver's seat and headed into the woods without saying a word.

I followed silently, my footsteps absorbed in a damp green carpet of ferns and mosses. With the sound of the wind, the hair on my arm brushed by a wet branch, a fluttering overhead, I was no longer a spectator, but joined in a communion of forest and earth. What gift could be so certain, so abundant, so generous and consistent? Could I call it mother, master, healer, friend? It soaked

PoeTTree

into me beyond words, an eternal memory of life at its finest, as it should be, here on the Oregon coast, where moisture sings its beautiful song.

Off in the distance I heard a mesmorizing flute music. It brought me out of my reverie and I observed the trees more closely. All of them were new growth, no more than ten or twenty years old. Suddenly, a sadness gripped me. Loggers had been through here and felled all of the giants from the ancient mountain top. The flute music spoke of a chilling history, and led me through a mass grave, covered over by time, and yet haunted still by the ghosts of those stricken titans. The fog swirled through the thin trunks of the secondary growth and I followed it onward, to the source of the music and the promise of a magnificent survivor. Up ahead I saw Eric, flute at his lips, eyes closed in concentration, playing his homage to a tree unlike any I had seen before.

Here stood a tree of unknown species. I couldn't mark it a Douglas Fir or Western Red Cedar, though it was likely one or the other. This tree seemed to have been placed here, as if a seed had drifted on a high wind from Sumatra, Bhutan or the Congo. Even more exotic, more unusual, perhaps delivered to earth by an ancient comet, or the washed up remnant of a primordial sea, crossed in the tide with a many-legged mollusk. Its trunk had the girth of ten mountain manatee back to belly. Twenty or thirty huge limbs gushed from the trunk just above the ground and reached straight into the rain clouds. Powder-green strands of moss dangled from its limbs and covered its bark. It almost sighed in the sponge and

PoeTTree

soak of the dripping interplay of life and mystery in and around it. This was an elder, wise beyond measure, powerful in its place as the only survivor, the one that made it and in so doing, seemed to hold every lost brother and sister in its mighty branches.

Eric's youth and beauty curled with his flute song up into the thick branches as a prayer rising to the dome of a temple. To see this young man, so taken with a tree, knowing as I did of his troubled past, brought it even higher in my esteem. Who can say what it did for him, what sort of anchor it provided his storm-tossed life? Here he was, now its ambassador, returning his gratitude by sharing its story. He ended his flute music, eyes filled with tears, and the power of story carried him forward: "This is the story of a tree, told and retold, and now given again to you . . . . Ten years ago, when I was eleven, my mother and father and I walked in the woods together, enjoying the trees and the streams and the beauty that we have always cherished living close to the land. We came to this very tree we are standing with now, and noticed a big red X painted on the trunk." I was chilled again as I had been before. I couldn't help but envision the millions of European Jews, marked in a similar way with the Star of David.

Eric continued: "This whole area of the forest was full of trees marked to be cut down." I saw my people, walking the streets of Warsaw and Berlin, marked like the trees, innocent, uncertain, their lives in the hands of some hidden power. Eric went on. "My family loved this tree. The people of our community loved this tree. Generations had come to honor and delight in its rare appearance.

There was no hesitation. We banded together to save it. Family and friends gathered in the night. Under lamps and flashlights people picked at the X in the bark. With scissors, tweezers, fingernails and knife blades we removed every speck of red paint. Whatever we had that could remove the mark of destruction was brought forward to save our tree." I thought of Europeans who had done the same for their Jewish neighbors. They hid them in walls and barns and secret compartments. Removed their marks and helped them into Switzerland or America.

PoeTTree

Eric concluded: "As the morning light arrived, we smeared mud on the bark, covering up any remaining trace of red, and went back down the mountain. I bring you here to appreciate this tree and share in the story of how it survived." I could not hold back my tears. In this odd and spectacular tree, an entire culture of wilderness remained vibrant. This tree did hold all of its brothers and sisters in its arms, just as the Holocaust survivors held their people in their onward beating hearts. I sat among the wet delicate ferns and loved this tree as Eric did, as all of his people did, for the hope it inspired in them.

This tree did not belong in the lumberyard. It belonged here, in this symphony of sound, the dripping abundance of nature, a poetic tree, branches spread across the sky, singing the epic verse of its heroic journey. One day it too will bow down and return to the soil, but will live without end in the stories that are shared.

Autumn

Elixir

Luminous saffron wings

Summer's captured sunlight

Glowing from every vein and stem

Blazing forth to warm the soul

Colorful Cottonwood

Astounding Aspen

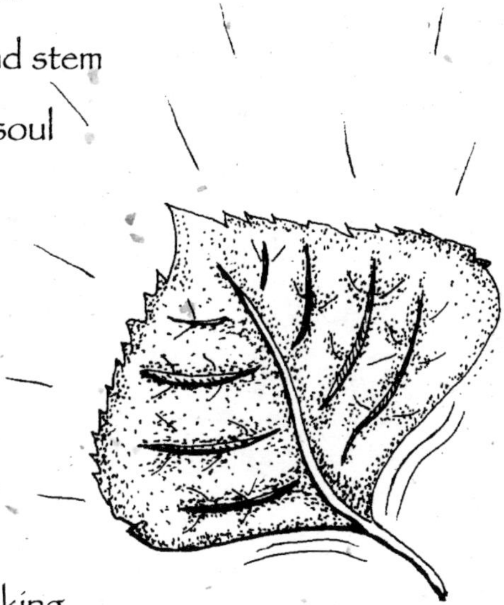

Quivering

Quaking

Fluttering

Flaming

PoeTTree

Fall golden passion

Dancing on a curtain of deep azure sky

Fill your soul!

Delight your Heart!

Ignite your Joy!

Savor Nature's Crowning Celebration!

Drink the Autumn Elixir!

PoeTTree

Tree
Tracks

I felt really good! Sweaty, dusty, aching good! A tray of tree
seedlings lay on the ground next to me. I crunched the shovel
through dry soil, small rocks, decayed plants, down into the moist
and welcoming earth, each treasured digging bringing me deeper
into history. Participating first hand in the future of this forest
delighted my soul! Down on my knees, I reached over and coaxed a
green infant seedling from its cradle. Before placing the tree into
the hole, I recalled the words of my tree planting buddy Gregory
Long, who said to tickle the roots and invite their mirthful expansion deep into the ground. I tickled the tree, but it was me that
smiled! The awaiting embrace of Mother Earth welcomed this
precious gift with openness. I planted and caressed the soil
around the tiny trunk with words of blessings on my lips. My
fingers carved a circular moat and I understood the fragility of
life—both the tree's and mine—each of us dependent upon the
generosity of the clouds.

Once again, as I had done so many times that day and thousands
of times over the years, I reached into the five-gallon bucket of
mulch and formed a bank of protection and nourishment around
the sapling. One more gift had been returned to this thirteen-acre
logging parcel that had been clear cut before—with the exception
of two soaring Lodgepole Pines. I could see in their towering pride
what this forest had once been, and what it might be again. Each

seedling planted would have these elders to show the way. I gave many of the trees I planted names, in honor of one of my friends or something that moved me about this planting site. "This one's name is Matilda," I heard a comrade say, developing the same attachment as me to each new life we tended.

That day we were all part of Fort Collins ReLeaf, an organization I cofounded, dedicated to planting and celebrating trees in Northern Colorado. This was my way of returning a favor. My greeting card company had spread joy to millions of people on the wings of trees who had given their lives to carry messages of love. To me the hundreds of hours I spent with ReLeaf was but a small gesture of appreciation for the gifts I had received from the forest. Joyfully, we brought thousands of excited and enthusiastic people into the forest and city parks, and planted close to thirty thousand trees.

That day in the clear-cut section of the forest, I stopped my planting and became aware of the others around me digging, planting, smoothing, mulching, watering, talking, and laughing. I saw families with youngsters, elders, young men and women, a community of industrious souls serving the forest. We had given them basic instructions about planting depth, spreading roots deep into the hole, watering and mulching. For the most part, however, we trusted each person's instincts. As I watched them work, I noticed some alone, others in groups. Some dug deep, others shallow.

PoeTTree

Each found his or her own way, and so contributed a unique blessing to the saplings he or she touched. There were as many right
ways as there were people, and each knew in a deep and soulful
way what it was the forest needed of them that day.

The cool breeze and white clouds swirling over the Rocky Mountains signaled our planting day was nearing completion. We all
knew that soon the snows of winter would come and the new life
we had planted would sleep under a cold white blanket and wait for
the warmth of spring. And then they would grow. As I began to
walk back to the seedling distribution area with about a dozen tiny
trees in my tray, I noticed a deep moose track imprinted in the soil.
In the stark light of day features had blended in, but here was a
rounded track now visible by the shadow cast upon its depth. I
knelt down and hollowed the compressed earth moose print,
reached for a tree and tucked it in, moved to the next track and
the next until the tray was empty. The moose had begun our tree
planting long before any of us had arrived and became a prophesy
of the rich diversity that would some day occupy this land. I could
feel the dew dripping from needles of tall trees. I could hear the
songs of birds, the wind's dancing through the branches and my
boots' crunch on pine cones. I could feel the bright mushrooms,
smooth and delicate in the moist shadows. All of this came to me in
the simple wandering of a moose, and I understood how all of us
are making furrows on the earth as we walk our paths, creating
places for mystery to root. I could also see that those who lived in

PoeTTree

harmony and loved this earth made tracks, beckoning me and others to plant beauty in their expectant hollows.

Three years later, I returned to our planting site. It was as if we were all still there. I could see the smiling faces and the dirty hands, shovels over shoulders, the same swirling clouds overhead. My soft tears fell to the ground, a grateful contribution to what had become in three years a sea of wispy green. There was Keith and Gloria and Richard and—yes, yes it is—Little Matilda a full two feet tall! The towering guardian trees that remained, and the surrounding forest, seemed to be proud of having witnessed the success of youth. I sat amid the vivid toddlers and imagined them in ten, fifteen, even a hundred years. They might not live that long, but their children would. And if we cared for the forest as those sweet volunteers had three years before, the trees would continue to propagate for thousands and thousands of generations.

I imagined, too, in my time there in the young forest how many stories had come from our day of planting. Each person had been touched in some way and had told others. An oral tradition may have formed for some, a sort of seed-planting in young minds that would surely feed the vision of an eternally beautiful woodland. For me, it was moose tracks. For someone else it may have been a shape in the clouds or the echo of a once meandering stream. For all of us it was something. I have no doubt of this.

PoeTTree

And so it is when one plants trees.

I Am
the
Tree of Life

Firmly rooted
Deeply committed
Completely nourished by the soil of my ancestors

Committed to this place
This BEAUTIFUL
Magnificent earth, Heavenly sky
Each precious butterfly, sunrise,
Every changing and precious moment of awe.

I live with joy of the seasons
Winter's fresh breath exhilaration
Growth and expansion of emerald green spring
The play-fullness of sweet summer's elixir
Autumn's letting go, return home.

From where I am rooted,
I look around.
I see the children of spring
I feel the power of summer
I love the renewal of winter
I know the truth of autumn

I draw energy up from the earth
Pulsing through my every limb and branch.
Radiating forth to share with community.
The forest is good and green and without it
The winds blow too strong,
Tearing my roots.
Questioning too strongly my tender connection.

Rain falls,
Yet another gift from mystery.
The greatest circle of life.

I breathe, and sway with honor,
Quiet enough to look around and appreciate all that is.
I stay
Rooted to where I belong.
To where
I long to be.

I am the Tree.
I am the Tree of Life.
I am

Dancing
to the
Earth

I was enjoying a fall walk along the Spring Creek bike path in Fort Collins. It was a beautiful blue-sky day, calm as could be. The kind of day that makes you feel blessed just to be alive. As I approached a big tree growing out of the riverbank, I noticed a few yellow leaves were fluttering through the sky and touching lightly on the ground. A few more steps nearer the tree and suddenly a shower of thousands of leaves filled the sky on their way to the earth. I was in the middle of a leaf downpour! As the leaves lay all around me, I felt deeply touched. From that place of connection inside me I instinctively knew that as each leaf let go of the branch in its final gesture of the season prayers of gratitude were released and I was showered with grace. The winds of some-thing much greater touched my life and so I share with you this poem.

PoeTTree

Dancing

to

the

Earth.

Letting Go.

Giving Thanks for Their Season.

Each   One   a   Prayer

of   Gratitude,

Beauty,

Trust.

Leaves

Dancing

Dancing

Dancing

Dancing to the Earth.

Showering Us with Prayers.

"All of
Nature
is a
Celebration!"

Tree Stories
from
Friends

Redwood Mystery

Rabbi Zalman Schachter-Shalomi

In Muir Woods in California there is a slice from a trunk of a more than two-thousand-year-old Redwood tree that had been sawed through and through. There is a legend beside it pointing to rings showing when great historic events occurred. The rings are not even. Those who know these things can tell about the climate in the years each one of these rings was shaped. As I stood there and looked, I felt something shift in me.

I had often in my kitchen sliced an onion and seen how in the onion and other vegetables the rings evolve from the center out—not so in a tree. The tree grows from the growing edge. The inner rings are from the youth of the tree and the outer ones are from the recent past. So every year a new ring begins at that growing edge. It is between the wood of last year's ring and the outer bark. I had learned that where the redwoods are concerned an occasional fire was an important way to stimulate new growth.

So here I was looking at that Sequoia and looking at the awesome mystery of the rings, of the way in which that tree had been witness to so much history. The vital membrane of the meeting of the environment and the tree was in the growing edge. What is most alive in the tree is not its center. In some way the tree could not accommodate new growth like an onion. The center of the tree is the hardest, the least flexible, the driest, the least juicy part. It could not allow each year for the inner core to issue new life without strangling it. The inner core of the tree was too set, too static. Yet this very quality is also the strength of the tree. The growing edge alone could not hold it up to stand rooted, enduring storms and weather. But the growing edge carries the life from the roots to the leaves and back. And yet the knotholes from which the branches issue forth go toward the center, the place where the growing edge was when the branch first sprouted.

When a tree dies, it is the growing edge that has died first. No more juice is raised from the roots, no more leaves the next year.

PoeTTree

It is sad to see a sturdy tree lose its life . . . . I thought of how we as persons grow. Here too our encounters with the outer world stimulate the new ring of experience on the tree of our lives. What tells me most about myself and the way in which I grow in the world is neither my past nor my present outer possessions. It is the vital growing edge, the place where I am vulnerable and alive, where what happens on the outside impinges on me, and where I digest and assimilate what happens on the outside. There too flows the nourishment from roots and leaves and the effect of the sunshine that comes to the roots.

Trees and people have a healthy growing edge. The tree of tradition gets its strength from the core and the past. It endures the storms and stands rooted. And it needs the growing edge of periodic renewal lest it die.

Spruce Tree's Promise

by Kathy Gatewood-Greenbank

Spruce Tree's best friend, Bird, would be leaving today for her warm southern home. It made Spruce sad to think of spending the long winter alone. Even the gently falling snow and crisp, cold air weren't cheering him up.

"Good morning, Spruce," Bird sang from her nest high up in Spruce's branches. "Isn't it a beautiful morning?"

"Yes it is, Bird." Spruce tried to sound lighthearted. "Are you ready for your flight south? I hope this snow won't delay you another day."

"I don't think it will. I'll be ready in a few minutes. I should have left last week, but I will miss you so much, I wanted to stay a little longer."

Bird paused for a moment." You will take care of my nest, won't you, Spruce?" Spruce smiled. "Yes, Bird. I promise I will keep it safe until you return."

Bird sang her thanks and her goodbye as she spiraled around Spruce. Then she turned and winged for the warm southern regions. Spruce whispered, "I love you, Bird. I'll see you in the spring."

Spruce remembered when Bird had first nested in his upper branches two summers ago. It seemed they had been friends longer than two years. Now it was October again and Bird was on her way. But he knew she would return in the spring as she had the last two years.

Spruce watched Bird until he could no longer see her against the brightness of the snow. Spruce was sorry to see Bird leave in the late fall, but he always looked forward to her return in the spring. Spruce was still thinking about Bird when he heard an unfamiliar sound. Crunch. Crunch. Crunch. Crunch.

Spruce's heart jumped. He looked around. He moved his branches slightly. He still couldn't see anything. The sound was coming closer. Crunch. Crunch. Crunch. Crunch.

Then Man stepped out from behind a tall tree. Spruce's heart was beating hard. Should he be frightened, he wondered. Man had not been in the forest for many years.

PoeT Tree

Man was carrying a strange looking stick over one shoulder and a coiled rope in his other hand. It was the stick that made Spruce nervous. It had a broad, almost flat piece of metal on one end.

Man stopped and smiled when he saw Spruce Tree. Then he started walking around Spruce. Crunch. Crunch. Crunch went Man's boots on the new snow. He walked all the way around Spruce, admiring the blue-green of Spruce's almost perfect cone shape.

"You're just what I've been looking for," Man said as he laid down his pack and the stick.

Spruce didn't understand what Man meant. Now Man was tying the rope around Spruce's branches, holding them up instead of spread out like they're supposed to be.

Spruce knew he should be afraid. He wanted to ask Man what he was doing. He wanted to know why he was being tied up.

Man picked up the stick and put the broad, flat end into the ground at Spruce's base. He pulled back on the stick and lifted a clod of dirt out of the ground. Then he did it again, next to the first spot. Then again, moving around Spruce.

"He's digging me up!" The thought exploded in Spruce's mind like lightening during a summer storm.

"Wait! You can't do this. I'll die!" Spruce tried to shriek at Man.

Then Spruce thought of Bird. "Bird is gone. When she returns I won't even be here. How can I keep my promise to keep her nest safe?" Spruce began to weep as Man kept on digging. No more would Spruce hear Bird's morning song. No more would he taste the clean, cold spring rains. Never again would he be able to stretch his branches and fan the small animals that lived on the forest floor.

Spruce suddenly realized Man had finished digging and had laid him gently on the snow-covered ground. Man was talking to Spruce as he took something out of his pack.

"I know you like the forest, Spruce Tree, but I want you to come live in my yard. It's very near here, at the edge of the forest. I'll wrap the bulb of your roots with this scrap of burlap to keep them safe until I get you home." Man looked at the nest in Spruce's top

PoeTTree

branches. "I'll wrap that nest, too. Maybe the bird will return."
Spruce could hardly believe his ears.

I'm not going to die, he thought. Man is taking me to his home. It's
so close, Bird will find me when she returns. Spruce thought his
heart might burst with joy.

Then a movement caught Spruce's eye. Man was taking something
else out of his pack. He knelt down where Spruce had been in the
ground. Very tenderly, Man took three tiny Spruce seedlings out
of another burlap bag.

PoeTTree

Man planted the frail sprigs where Spruce had once cast his
shadow and cooled his forest friends.

As Man carefully wrapped bits of burlap around the base of each
seedling, he said, "I'm taking tree from the forest for my pleasure,
so I'm replacing it with three new trees for the forest's pleasure."

Spruce felt a happy tear slide from his eye. The sun broke
through the clouds and made the snow sparkle. Spruce Tree's
future looked very bright.

As he was being moved to his new home, he again thought of Bird.
She will find me in the spring. I will keep my promise to her. Her
nest will be safe.

And Spruce Tree knew Bird, Man and himself would be friends for
many years to come.

Plant a Tree-
Grow a Friend

Song Lyrics
by Sheldon Sands & Ilan Shamir

When we plant a tree we grow a friend.
A friend we'll have for life,
a friend we'll have for life.
When we plant a tree we grow a home,
A home for birds, bees, for lovers and sweet things.

A friend to stand by us through all,
give us cool, relaxing shade,
Give us shelter from the wind and the rain.
Give us air that's fresh and pure,
With changing colors through the year,
'This and more from our true tree friends.

PoeTTree

When we plant a tree we seed a prayer,
And we send it to the earth and the stars.
When we plant a tree we raise a branch
Our children may climb after we've moved from here.

PoeTTree

A friend to stand by us through all,
give us cool, relaxing shade,
Give us shelter from the wind and the rain.
Give us air that's fresh and pure,
With changing colors through the year,
'This and more from our true tree friends.

I'd like to be more like a tree,
a friend to every being.
Strong and tall and swaying with the breeze,
My feet dug into the earth,
Head and arms held high to the sky,
the stars and the sun.

A friend to stand by us through all,
give us cool, relaxing shade,
Give us shelter from the wind and the rain.
Give us air that's fresh and pure,
With changing colors through the year,
'This and more from our true tree friends.

PoeTTree

Invocation
for Earth Day
Tree Planting

By Katharine Gregory

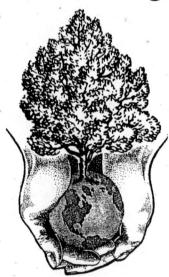

Planet Earth
Mother Earth
Living Earth
Gaia

We break into your rich, dark skin
not thoughtlessly,
but with gratefulness and care.

Shoveling,
digging deep,
we listen and open ourselves
to the magic of your springtime cycle.

As you receive these roses, junipers, red twig dogwoods
into your soil,
Let us learn from you
how to nurture seemingly small things,
Such as
each other
and hope.

PoeTTree

Teach us even just a little
about how you nourish these green living beings.
How you surround them,
yet give them space.
How you pay attention to them
and urge their roots to take hold and spread.

Planet Earth
Mother Earth
Living Earth
Gaia
Teach us how to give back to you,
protect you, nourish you.
Let us learn from you how to nurture our own dreams
like saplings, full of promise.

Beginnings and Endings

Martha McClennen-Stapp

I will tell a story as I once heard it . . .

It was a cold night and the friends gathered close around the fire. The fire and their friendship both warmed them and they spent many hours laughing and talking and sharing their love. In the fire they burned a piece of an old wooden bowl that they had found upon the wood pile out back, and this story is about the life of that bowl and the death that it now faced . . .

Once upon a time, many, many years ago, in the early spring a
tender shoot was planted beside the cabin. It was the first tree
that they had planted by their new home and they watched it and
watered it as it grew over the years.

Ten years passed, and the tree grew and in the summer became the
favorite shady spot for the cat to lie on hot days and dream of the
birds landing above. A few more years passed, a child was born
and grew, and one day went with his father to build a swing from
the branches. The child loved the swing and the tree and spent
many hours playing games and creating roles for the tree. Sometimes it was a fortress, sometimes a living plant, and sometimes a
sailing ship. Again the years passed, and the child grew to be a
young man, and as young men will do, he used to sneak kisses with
his sweetheart under that tree beneath the summer moon.

Well, the young man left that home to seek his life, and his parents
grew old. Before he left he built a bench beneath the tree where
they could sit and rest and enjoy the breeze. And again more
years passed, and first the husband and then the wife passed on,
and when they did their ashes were spread beneath the tree and
nourished it and it grew very large.

A new couple then came to live there and they also loved the tree.
When they first moved in they planted daffodils in a circle around
the tree to watch each spring. But in their first winter in that home
there was a great storm. The rain and wind pounded the house for

hours that night, and there was much crashing as branches and trees were whipped about. In the morning when they awoke, they discovered that the tree had blown down.

So the next day, the man went and began to chop up the tree for firewood. And as he was chopping, a hobo came by and admiring the wood, asked if he might have a piece to carve. The hobo took the wood and began to carve a bowl. He worked for many days as he traveled and made a fine bowl, which he could eat from. He carried that bowl for many years on his journey and it became one of his most prized possessions.

One day, as the hobo was eating his dinner from the bowl, he heard the sound of many people and dogs coming along the river. He was frightened by this . . . as hobos aren't always popular, and so dropping the bowl and all the rest of his meager belongings, he ran away quickly to hide. When the dogs reached the place where the hobo had been, one of them found the bowl and finding that it still had food in it, he carried it off a ways to where he could eat undisturbed.

So then for many years the bowl sat quietly in the woods beside the river. And the rainwater would gather in the bowl, and the mice would come to drink from it. And once some animal nudged it over and for a while it became home for many little crawling bugs.

Then one day a young family came for a picnic beside the river. The little girl, who was always very mischievous, ran this way and

PoeTTree

that, playing in the woods. She jumped over logs and ducked behind trees, and finally tripped and fell right in front of the bowl. So she picked up the bowl and began to play games with it. She pretended that it was a hat for a while, and then floated it like a boat upon the river. And when the picnic was over she took the bowl home with her.

At home the bowl was added to the toys in the sandbox and spent many years, and many childhoods, being imagined into a whole array of adventures. But then all the children grew and the mother eventually began to use the bowl to store seeds for her garden. And one year, as she worked in her garden, she was startled by the sound of her son's voice—her son who had gone to fight in the war and now had returned—and she dropped the bowl and it broke in two. And in the excitement the bowl was forgotten and the pieces put in a corner in the garage.

Again, years passed and new people lived in the house, and as they sorted through the odds and ends and nooks and crannies, they found a piece of the bowl and added it to the woodpile. Then one night, when special friends were coming to visit, they built a fire and placed the broken piece of the bowl in the fire. And the fire blazed. And they sat together and shared their love. And there were no beginnings and no endings, only the warmth.

And so the story ends, and I guess what want to say is that the mystery of where we come from and where we go and what we do in between is a pattern so complex that I don't think I can ever know exactly what I have done, but hope that it brings warmth.

About the Author

Ilan Shamir was born and raised in San Antonio, Texas, in the beauty of bluebonnets, wildflowers, and Oak trees near the Texas hill country. Educated at Washington University in St. Louis, Missouri, his first work experiences led him to marketing and product design for 7Up-The Uncola, Pet, Inc., and Sunline brands. He left the corporate grid and nourished his love of wild beauty as a photographer and expedition leader in the Swiss Alps for Wilderness Travel. This culminated in a forty-day solo across remote Iceland, followed by time in Greenland.

His return to the states brought him to the mossy, dripping Northwest, and he fell in love with Oregon. The ocean, mountains and ancient trees sang a song that fed his soul. The green and growing fullness of Oregon inspired Ilan to germinate his own greeting card company in 1978. Each card contained a special gift of seeds, potpourri, herbal tea, cocoa or spices, and a heartfelt message about caring for the earth. The company has spread its unique and environmentally conscious message to some fifteen million people.

In homage to the trees that gave their lives to his card company, Ilan created Fort Collins ReLeaf in 1990 with Gregory Long. The organization has returned more than thirty thousand trees to the earth. Out of the plantings grew a unique approach to ritual and ceremony, and creative approaches such as "Treehenge" in Fort Collins, a living re-creation of Stonehenge in England.

Ilan has traveled to a Mexican village of the Huichol Indians, to study with the one-hundred-year-old shaman Don José Matsua, and a visionary yarn painter named Eligio Carrillo. The Huichol traditions as well as Jewish Mysticism, Kabalah, and Native American teachings are an important part of his daily spiritual practice.

He currently lives in Colorado, among the golden fluttering Aspen and uplifting Rocky Mountains with his wife Kris and daughter Laurel. Ilan creates personalized Soul Reflections to assist people on their spiritual journeys. These dazzling artworks and stories illuminate the individual's essence and inspire a deeper understanding of life. His time is rich with book writing, poetry, developing educational products for children and leading Kabalistic Tree of Life ceremonies.

Ilan views himself as a "Chameleon in a Crayola Box," inspired by the endless excitement in each new day!

PoeTTree

Also by Ilan Shamir

Books

Tree Celebrations!

Booklets

Planting and Caring for your Family Tree—
   the "hole" story!
Tree Celebrations!

Posters

Universal Bank & Trust
Plant a Tree—Grow a Friend
Ten Mitzvah

Greeting Cards

Greeting Seeds, Greeting Teas, Greeting Scents,
  Seasoned Greetings, Something Extra

To order call 1-800-992-4769
or email: IlanShamir@Juno.com

PoeTTree

"When You Plant a Tree,
You Grow a Friend,
A Friend You'll Have for Life!"

-Ilan Shamir

Acknowledgments

Fred Deneke
Andy Lipkis
Gregory Long
Pepper Provensano
Richard Seidman
Ray Trethaway
Tim Womick
Great tree-planting friends who have planted
millions of trees and a lot of hope

Stanley & Barbara Hammer
For the gift of a Magnolia Tree

Bill Shaw
Poet Laureate Shaw-Walden

Kris Baldwin
For her love and lots of help

James Churches & Mary Herrick
For their love of words and love of trees

Mom and Dad
For planting trees
in front of my elementary school

Frank Lockyear
My first tree-planting teacher

105

PoeTTree

Resources

There are many ways to become involved with Trees! The following resources are some of the best in the country and are ones I have been involved with personally. Becoming more involved as a member of a national or local organization is a great way to connect with other tree enthusiasts. Finding a new favorite tree book or connecting with some of the computer web sites can be exciting ways to "branch out" and "enjoy the view"!

Community Tree-Planting Organizations:

Friends of Trees- 2634 N.E. Martin Luther King Boulevard, Portland, Oregon 97212, 503-282-8846

Tree Utah- 364 E. Broadway, Salt Lake City, Utah 84111, 801-364-2122

TreePeople- 12601 Mulholland Drive, Los Angeles, California 90210, 818-753-4600

Sacramento Tree Foundation- 201 Lathrop Way, Suite F, Sacramento, California 95815, 916-924-8733

Tree New Mexico- P.O. Box 81827, Albuquerque, New Mexico 87198, 505-265-4554

Dallas Tree & Park Foundation- 2121 San Jacinto, Suite 1111, Dallas, Texas 75201, 214-953-1184, www.dallastpf.org

Trees Atlanta- 96 Poplar N.W., Atlanta, Georgia 30303, 404-522-4097

Trees, Water & People- 633 South Remington, Fort Collins, Colorado 80524, 970-484-3678

Alliance for Community Trees- PO Box 464, College Park, MD, 20741, 301-699-2203. Complete listing of all community tree organizations. See www.AcTrees.org listed below

Web Sites:

www.ReplantTrees.org - Plant trees for all the paper you or your business uses through this easy to use calculator

www.SpiritofTrees.org - Beautiful site celebrating trees and nature with wonderful pictures.

www.AcTrees.org - Alliance for Community Trees site. If you would like to find ways to become involved in tree planting or care in your local community or start a tree organization in your area this is a must see resource.

www.Treelink.org - A great site that has wonderful tree information as well as links to a lot of other very exciting and informative sites!

Books:

Tree Stories, A Collection of Extraordinary Encounters, Edited by Jacobs & Shragg

The Wisdom of Trees, Jane Gifford

The Thunder Tree, Robert Michael Pyle

The Attentive Heart-Conversations With Trees, Stephanie Kaza

The Giving Tree, Shel Silverstein

The Man Who Planted Trees, Jean Giono

Education of Little Tree, Forest Carter

Tree in the Trail, Holling, Clancy & Holling

Meeting With Remarkable Trees, Thomas Pakenham

Myths of the Sacred Tree, Moyra Caldecott

Fantastic Trees, Edwin Menninger

BeLEAF It or Knot!, Ilan Shamir

An Amazing Tree Enthusiast!:

Trail of Trees- c/o National Tree Trust, 1120 G Street N.W. Suite 770, Washington, D.C. 20005, 800-218-7245, www.nationaltreetrust.org. Tim Womick has been running and biking across and around the country for many years, sharing his amazing enthusiasm for trees with school kids!

Music:

"Plant a Tree-Grow a Friend" - Music by Sheldon Sands, lyrics by Sheldon Sands and Ilan Shamir. P.O. Box 410, Boulder Colorado 80306, email: SJsands@Hotmail.com

Educational Materials:

Tree Celebrations-Planting and Celebrating Trees with Ceremonies, Stories and Activities, P.O. Box 272309, Fort Collins, Colorado 80527, 800-992-4769, email: grow@yourtruenature.com

There are a wealth of other great tree resources. Use the
envelope included in the back of this book to send us your tree
story, poem, picture, experience, song . . . information on your
favorite tree book, web site . . . anything having to do with trees!
I would love to hear from you! Write or email to us at:

Ilan Shamir
Your True Nature, Inc.
PO Box 272309
Fort Collins, CO 80527
email: grow@yourtruenature.com
www.yourtruenature.com

The End

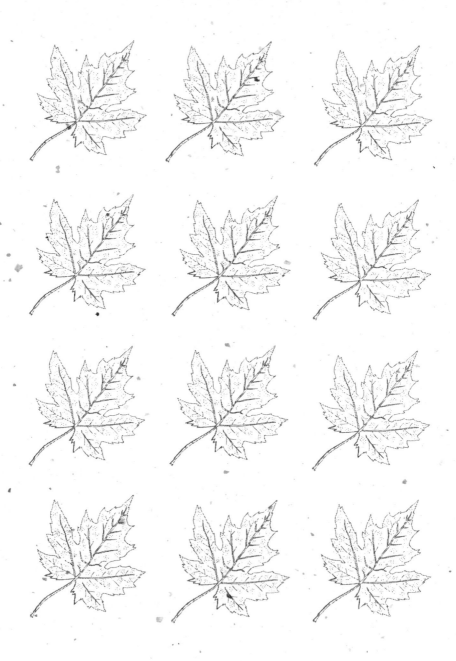

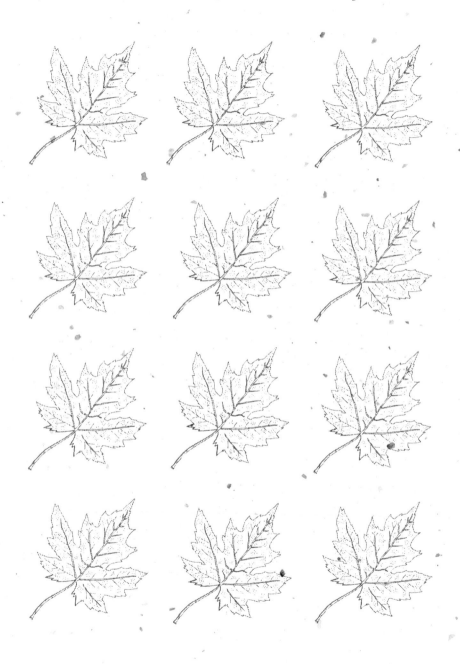